This book belongs to:

_____

Published by Ladybird Books Ltd
A Penguin Company
Penguin Books Ltd, 80 Strand, London WC2R 0RL, UK
Penguin Books Australia Ltd, Camberwell, Victoria, Australia
Penguin Books (NZ) Ltd, Cnr Airbourne and Rosedale Roads, Albany, Auckland, 1310, New Zealand

3 5 7 9 10 8 6 4 2

Printed in Italy

Knights

written by Lorraine Horsley
illustrated by Laszlo Veres

Ladybird

Knights were soldiers
who fought on horses
hundreds of years ago.

It took many years of hard
work to become a knight.

When a boy was seven
years old, he went to live
and work for a nobleman.

He became a page.

A nobleman was a rich and important person who lived in a castle.

A page learnt how to use a sword.

A page also learnt
how to use a
bow and arrow.

When a page was fourteen years old, he became a squire.

A squire learnt how to dress a knight in armour.

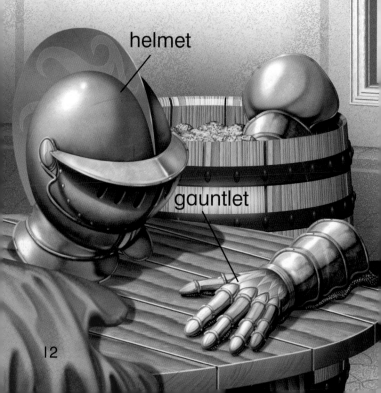

helmet

gauntlet

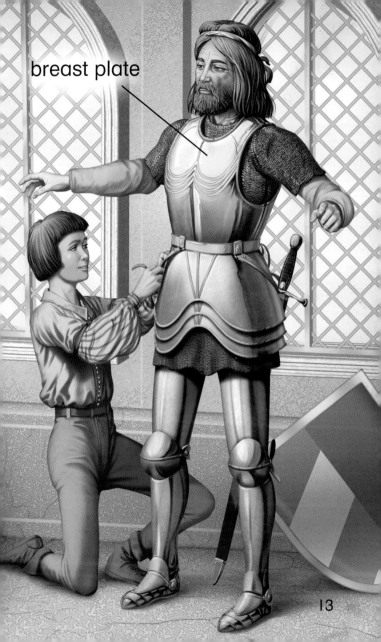

breast plate

A squire learnt how to serve and carve meat at the table.

Dinner was the biggest meal
of the day for rich people.
They ate soup, meat, fish
and bread.

A squire learnt how to look after horses and clean armour.

A squire had to clean the
armour in a barrel of sand.

A squire learnt how to fight and ride a horse.

lancing

wrestling

fencing

A squire learnt how to hunt.

Rich people hunted deer,
wolves, birds,
rabbits and
wild boar.

When a squire was
twenty-one years old,
he became a knight.

king

A knight had to serve the
king and fight for his country.

A knight had to fight in
special games.

This game was called
jousting.

Games, like jousting, helped a knight learn how to fight in a real battle.

A knight had to fight in battles for the king.

axe

sword

mace

Can you remember how the page became a knight?

page

squire grooming

squire fencing

squire hunting

squire becoming
a knight

knight

Index